The Secret World of Ants

An Exploration of an Underground Insect Species

Written by Štěpánka Sekaninová
Illustrated by Zuzana Dreadka Krutá

Sky Pony Press
New York

Contents

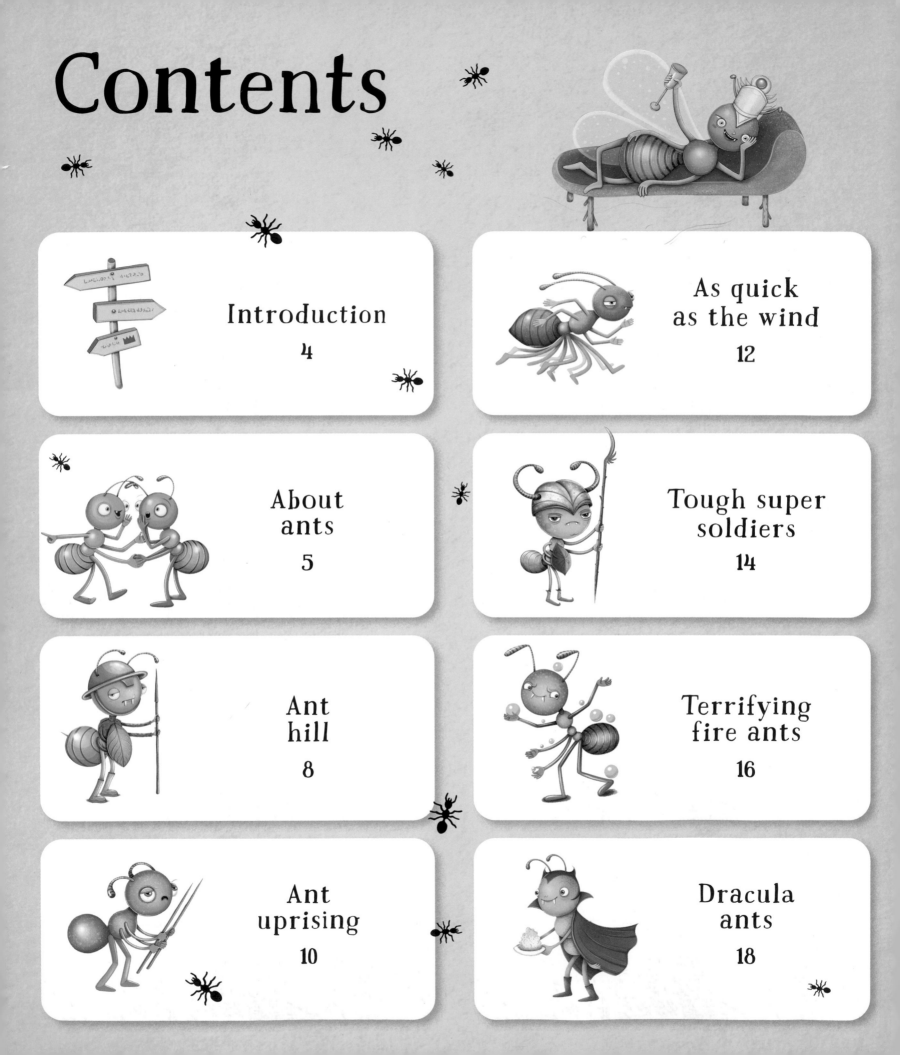

Introduction

You might think, "Ants, bah; why's there even a book about something so small and unimportant?" But you're wrong, children! Ants are the largest group of insects on the planet. Allegedly, anywhere from 25,000 to 35,000 ant species populate Earth, though scientists have only managed to document roughly half of them. Ant behavior and actions greatly influence natural ecosystems.

Related to bees and bumblebees, ants evolved 100 million years ago from wasps. Just like wasps, bees, and bumblebees, ants live in large colonies, which is why we call them social insects. Looking behind the curtain of the ant way of life, we can see that in some sense these crawlies are a lot like us humans.

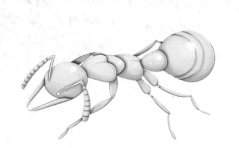

Prehistoric ant

They're excellent insect hunters and exterminators.

They remove dead animals, helping to keep nature clean.

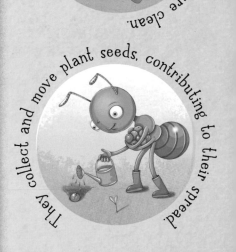

They collect and move plant seeds, contributing to their spread.

Ants that live under the ground loosen and aerate the soil.

Ant society

The queen is the most important member of any ant hill. These rulers are the mothers of the entire colony, diligently laying eggs and making sure the community doesn't go extinct and always has enough industrious worker ants at its disposal. A typical ant queen lives for up to twenty years.

Queen

You can easily tell her apart from the other ants because she is larger. In her youth, she has wings but breaks them off once fertilized by male ants.

Workers

The biggest group in the entire ant hill, some are in charge of maintaining and repairing the colony while other workers seek food and feed the queen. Another important group of workers takes care of eggs, pupae, and larvae.

Male ants

Winged male ants have an extremely short lifespan. They die as soon as they fulfill their life's mission—fertilizing the queen.

Worker soldiers

Equipped with frightening-looking mandibles, they protect the ant hill from predators and other threats.

Queen

Worker

Male ant

Worker soldier

Ant communication

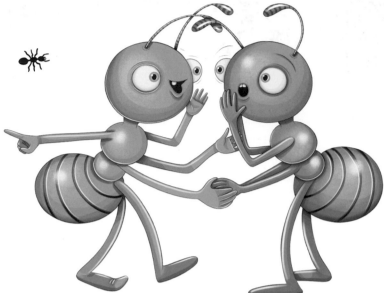

All senses at once

When two ants meet, they start communicating, using their sense of smell, taste, sight, touch, and hearing. In this way, two members of the same colony can safely recognize each other and convey significant information, such as where a source of tasty food is or if there's some danger lurking around.

Two ants are talking

When an ant is hungry

When a fed worker ant meets another worker that's hungry, what will it do? It'll share, by feeding the latter with its mouth. Besides exchanging nutrients, the adult ants also swap important news and information.

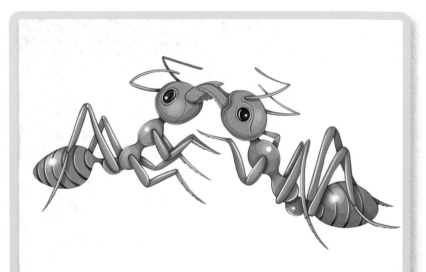

Adult worker feeds another worker

Body of an ant

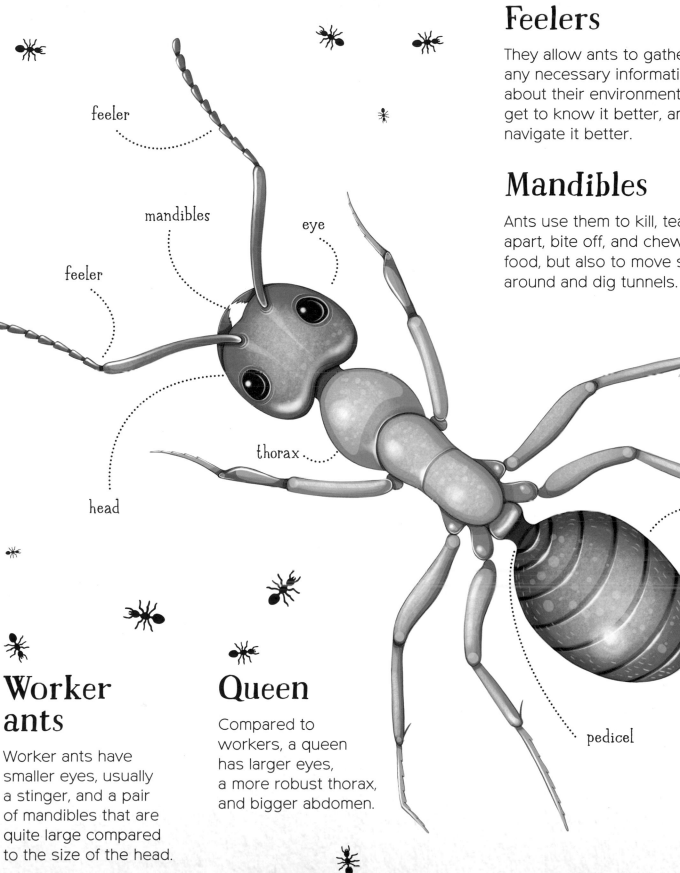

feeler

mandibles

eye

feeler

head

thorax

abdomen

pedicel

stinger

Feelers

They allow ants to gather any necessary information about their environment, get to know it better, and navigate it better.

Mandibles

Ants use them to kill, tear apart, bite off, and chew their food, but also to move stuff around and dig tunnels.

Worker ants

Worker ants have smaller eyes, usually a stinger, and a pair of mandibles that are quite large compared to the size of the head.

Queen

Compared to workers, a queen has larger eyes, a more robust thorax, and bigger abdomen.

Ant hill

Different ant species have different ways of life—some live in tree hollows, others under stones or in rock clefts, and yet other ones under the ground, on trees, or in ant hills. An ant hill is a much more intricate structure than you might have thought. In the dome is an elaborate network of ingeniously interconnected tunnels and chambers, reaching deep under the ground. Regardless of how cold it is outside, the ants enjoy the balmy 68°F (20°C) at home. To guarantee this, they build their hill, in a place with lots of sunlight and make certain its longest side faces the south. This ensures that the sun warms the ant hill which then accumulates the heat. The ants themselves also help heat up the hill. Worker ants scuttle out of the hill at the first spring light to bask in the sun. The heat they accumulate in their bodies also warms up the hill's interior.

Leave us alone—we're getting our tans.

Construction materials:

needles, twigs, dirt, sometimes even an entire tree stump

Having read this brief introduction to the life and appearance of ants, you can now set off for a great adventure among a few ant species. Some you might find funny, others perplexing, yet other ones frightening, and believe it or not, you will occasionally find yourself in places you'll want to run away from because of, to put it mildly, their life-threatening inhabitants. . . .

Well, you're not really resembling me right now.

Why resin?

We know that anthills are made of dirt, clay, needles, and twigs. If you take a more detailed look at an anthill, you will see that there are small fragments of resin in its corridors. Ants are well aware that resin protects their home against unwanted bacteria. For ants, resin is a perfect antibiotic.

Ant uprising

There are many ant species whose members enslave other ants. While wearing the scent of their victims, these ants sneak into the home of their marks, steal their pupae (which will later produce young enslaved ants), and then enslave hostages as well.

I enslave ants

1. Temnothorax americanus

I'm an enslaved ant.

2. Temnothorax

Get them!!!

But enslaved ants sometimes revolt. When they decide the time's right, the subjugated ants rise against their enslavers, destroy the pupae containing future enslaved queens, and raid the entire enslaver colony. "Hurray! We've won again," call the victorious ants after a successful revolt.

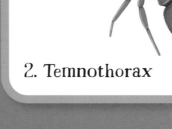

Look at them go.

1

Home in a tiny acorn

These ant enslavers are so small their whole colony fits inside a single acorn, comfortably housing everyone.

As quick as the wind

Members of this African ant species live in scorching deserts and could easily rival the greatest sprinters since they manage to run at the incredible speed of 2.2 miles (3.6 km) an hour. Oh no, don't you dare scoff! Converted to human speed, it means these talented ants would be able to run at 478 miles (770 km) per hour if human. They might as well be flying.

I'm floating here

If you look at the running ant closely, you might notice it's literally floating above desert sand—all of its six legs are in the air. This is the only way to prevent the hot sand from hurting the ant.

Running to survive

Desert ants have evolved their running style and speed in order to survive. The faster they manage to reach food in the form of dead animals, the shorter amount of time they spend exposed to the dangerous sun.

Faster, or the sun will bake me alive!

The cool underground is great, though.

I live in the desert.

Cataglyphis bombycina

Big-headed guardians

The entrance to the ant hill is being closely watched by well-built ants with large heads. And woe be to anyone who comes closer! Grab, crunch, gulp! The guardians will eliminate them. Strong mandibles are the best weapon the army has at its disposal. Before the enemies get their bearings, they're out of the fight, at best one leg, at worst a head shorter.

Thanks to these soldiers, I'm not afraid of a thing.

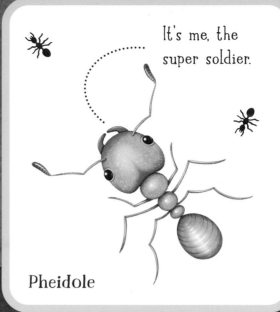

It's me, the super soldier.

Pheidole

The big head advantage

Ant warriors can use their huge heads to seal off all entrances, preventing the enemy from sneaking inside.

Ha, halt, not another step.

Tough super soldiers

Some ant queens have it made, sitting as they do in ant hills and laying one egg after another, barely facing any danger from the outside world! That's because they're protected by an army of huge super soldiers.

Terrifying fire ants

Help, a disaster has befallen us. Run away! Save yourselves! Anyone who has their wits about them is fleeing. From what? A huge array of the most feared predators in the world—the fire ants. They march forward, not taking pity on anything or anyone.

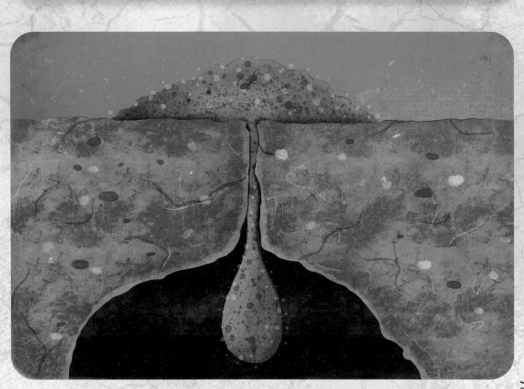

And now we'll turn into water ants

The fearsome fire ants can adapt to any environment, simply by changing their state —from solid to liquid. Yes, scientists have witnessed the ants literally pour through a narrow funnel, just like thick syrup.

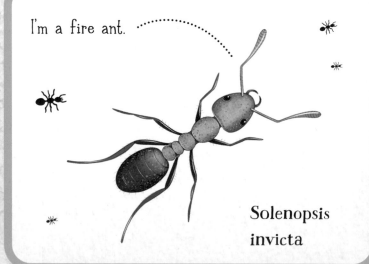

I'm a fire ant.

Solenopsis invicta

Water ahead

No obstacle can stop them. There's an endless water course spanning ahead? No problem! They immediately form a raft with their bodies and get to the opposite bank. It doesn't matter that the voyage can take up to fourteen days.

Help, fire ants!

People, too, are afraid of fire ants as they can destroy harvests, eliminate farm animals, and disrupt the foundations of houses by digging long underground passages.

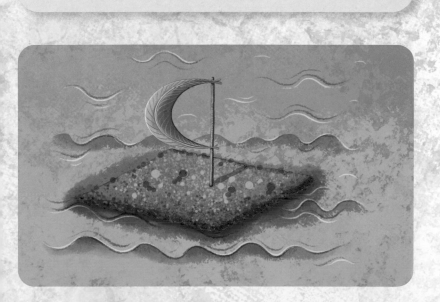

Dracula ants

They may be tiny and seem inconspicuous but in fact are the world's speed record holders and manage to outperform even the cheetah itself. We're talking about an Australian ant species whose members can move their mandibles at an incredible speed. The movement is so rapid you can't perceive it with the naked eye—it's 5,000 times as quick as the blink of an eye.

As strong as a bull

Despite being amazingly fast, the jaws of these ants are exceptionally strong. Other ants have quite a lot of catching up to do.

Ah, sweet, sweet blood

And why are they named after the famous vampire? Probably because in order to eat, they must first feed their larvae. Once they do, they bite a hole in the stuffed larvae and suck their blood. Don't worry, they don't do this because they're evil; they just can't digest solid foods.

Come have a bite, girls.

Diligent weavers

"Hold onto the leaves, friends, so that I can sew them together. Or would you prefer spending the night out in the open?" say large, strong workers as they link up to form a loooong chain and drag over a couple of leaves, roll them together, and hold onto them. Then a couple of smaller workers hurry over, carrying larvae with them—a source of thread.

I'm a weaver.

Oecophylla smaragdina

Successful animal farming

Weaver ants are also quite skilled farmers of aphids and blue butterfly caterpillars. They protect them against hornets and wasps. In turn, the critters give them the sweet juice of their bodies. Weaver ants also eliminate insects that harm fruit trees.

worker with aphid larvae

aphid

No disturbing, I'm sewing

The ant in charge of the sewing itself holds a larva in its mandibles, jumping over the gap in the leaves while gently tapping the larva's head to make it excrete what will become a thread. The result? A perfect nest that's safely hidden up in a tree.

Atta ants

Buzz off, we're in a hurry, have no time to waste, need to cut stuff up. Atta ants never know a moment of peace. Large workers of this species run around tropical forests, cut pieces of leaves off trees, and bring them into their ant hill. There, a crowd of smaller workers is awaiting them. One group licks the leaves to remove any dirt and then shreds them. The final group chews these pieces and stores them in their mushroom grow houses inside the ant hill.

Yummy, mushrooms

Along with leaf sap, the cherished mushrooms are an important source of food for the Atta ants, one without which they wouldn't be able to survive.

When I was young, I could cut down the whole forest.

My mandibles are starting to hurt.

Ant and retired

When older ants wear out their mandibles so much they're no longer capable of cutting off a single piece of leaf, they go into retirement. It's an active one, though, as they still help bring cut-up leaves inside the ant hill.

Let them grow

The ants take good care of the harvest in their grow houses. They weed it regularly, carefully remove any unhealthy mushroom fibers, and shower the entire growth with secretions to prevent fungal infections. Clearly, they're quite experienced gardeners.

I enjoy cutting things.

Atta

23

Dangerous queen

Ants are no creatures of peace. For example, there are ant queens that select a foreign ant hill and start hanging around until they spot an opportunity to sneak in among the unsuspecting worker ants.

It's me, the dangerous queen.

1. Temnothorax stumperi

I won't allow you to assail me like this.

2. Leptothorax tuberum

Yeah, yeah, I'll get your throne in no time.

When a foreign worker notices her, the queen plays dead.

Once the worker calms down, the queen climbs onto her back and adopts her scent.

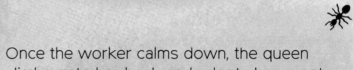

In this way, she is taken directly to the other queen and unseats her.

From now on, she's the one ruling the conquered colony.

Honeypot ants

Darn, this is so heavy! I mean, you try going around with a butt that's bigger than you are, and so heavy—so heavy because it's packed with sweet nectar. Yup, certain honeypot ants collect nutritious honeydew in their butts (a.k.a. their abdomens) to help their comrades survive in hungry times.

Stocking up

These stock providers either get their honeydew from aphids or collect it directly from acacia trees. Other ants, too, can add some for safekeeping. After all, they know very well there may come a time when the stores in their mates' butts can save their lives. All they need to do then is find the nearest full abdomen and drink up. Yummy, so good.

Those ants are taking such good care of me.

All right, niiice. The more nectar the better; this winter's going to be hard.

My abdomen is full of honeydew.

Myrmecocystus mimicus

27

Raider ants

Some ants are quite crafty little fellows. They can enslave other ants without breaking a sweat. First, they send a commando unit of four to infiltrate an ant hill that was chosen in advance. The four commandos camouflage themselves with the scent of their enemies to stay off the radar. Fantastic. Once they're invisible like this, they grab any larvae and pupae they stumble upon and take them home. Great work, everyone.

Uh-oh, a fight's a-brewing

Sometimes the ants being invaded notice the infiltrators roaming about. That's quite bad . . . for them. The raiders start fighting them, and there can be no doubt they're excellent warriors, capable of sticking their stingers directly into their enemies' delicate necks. The outcome? A clear victory for the raiders, with no losses among their own!

I'm a raider.

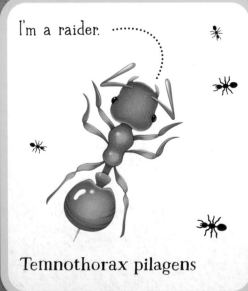

Temnothorax pilagens

29

30

Terrifying decorations

Paying a visit to certain ant hills can be quite a horrible experience. That's because some ants decorate their homes with the severed heads of their enemies. How awful! Especially since those severed heads belong to bold warriors equipped with strong mandibles.

Uh oh, a pirate has arrived!

Tried-and-tested trick

Decorating your nest with the heads of your enemies is just a survival tactic. The ants adopt the scent of the feared predators that are now decorating their walls and gain protection against future ant raiders—especially the ant pirates. The scent of ants with huge mandibles stops any raiding attempt in its infancy. Quite a smart way to save one's skin, don't you think?

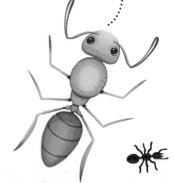

We'll fend off any pirate.

1. Formica archboldi

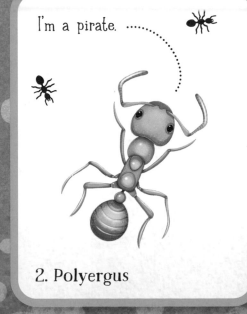

I'm a pirate.

2. Polyergus

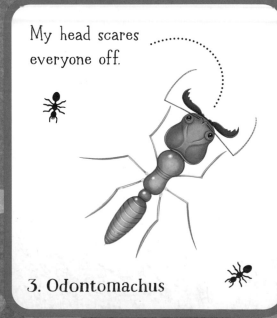

My head scares everyone off.

3. Odontomachus

Ant rafters

There are ants who just love water. They love it so much they live on river banks as a matter of principle. Not even floods are a problem for them. If one comes, they link their bodies together to form floating rafts and brave the high waters.

I'm the important one; how about you?

Did you know there's a special seating arrangement on the ant raft? It's determined by the station and age of the individual ants. If they take care of larvae, they're important and get to occupy one of the safer places. But if they're old and weak, they obediently go to the riskier sections, ready to sacrifice themselves for the others.

I'm a proud rafter.

Formica selysi

Finally, high water! Let's go rafting.

The worker ants are scattered across the width of the raft and form a protective dome around the queen.

Save the queen!

The raft's floor consists of larvae and pupae which, unlike the adult ants, can easily stay afloat. Once the raft reaches the bank, the workers fish out any larvae or pupae that got separated during the journey, saving them. Most importantly, though, the queen was kept safe—the entire point of the ant vessel in the first place.

Conquering the castle

Put some grease into it, girls. We need to dig our way into the ant hill as soon as possible! "I'm hungry, and my knees are buckling," one of the small yet quite aggressive worker ants might call out if it were a human. That's because the workers of this species dig underground corridors to reach the ant hills of other ant species.

Keep digging, I'm right behind you

Taking it all

As soon as the invaders reach their destination, they grab reinforcements, and a fierce fight breaks out. The invaders begin spraying secretions in the ant hill to confuse the defenders. As the commotion rages, they burst into the enemy's pantries and chambers containing larvae, pupae, and eggs and snatch everything they stumble across.

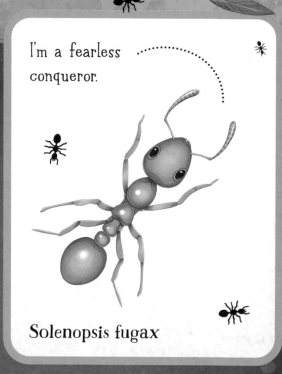

I'm a fearless conqueror.

Solenopsis fugax

A conqueror attacks . . .

. . . with special secretions.

Back off, rivals

Oh no, seems like my privileged position in the ant hill is in danger! Certain ant species need to worry about being overthrown. So as soon as this idea occurs to the ant who's occupying a significant position in the ant hill, along with the queen, it attacks its rival without a second thought, seizing it with its mandibles and covering it with lethal secretions to make sure there will be no exchange of power!

Off with the young

A power-thirsty ant has all bases covered and will attack even the tiny little ants that have just emerged from their pupae, engaging them in a fierce battle. The younglings have no chance. The offending ant knows very well that if it waited just a little while, the young ants would eventually grow wings and become much stronger opponents.

Oh dear, this is the tenth one today.

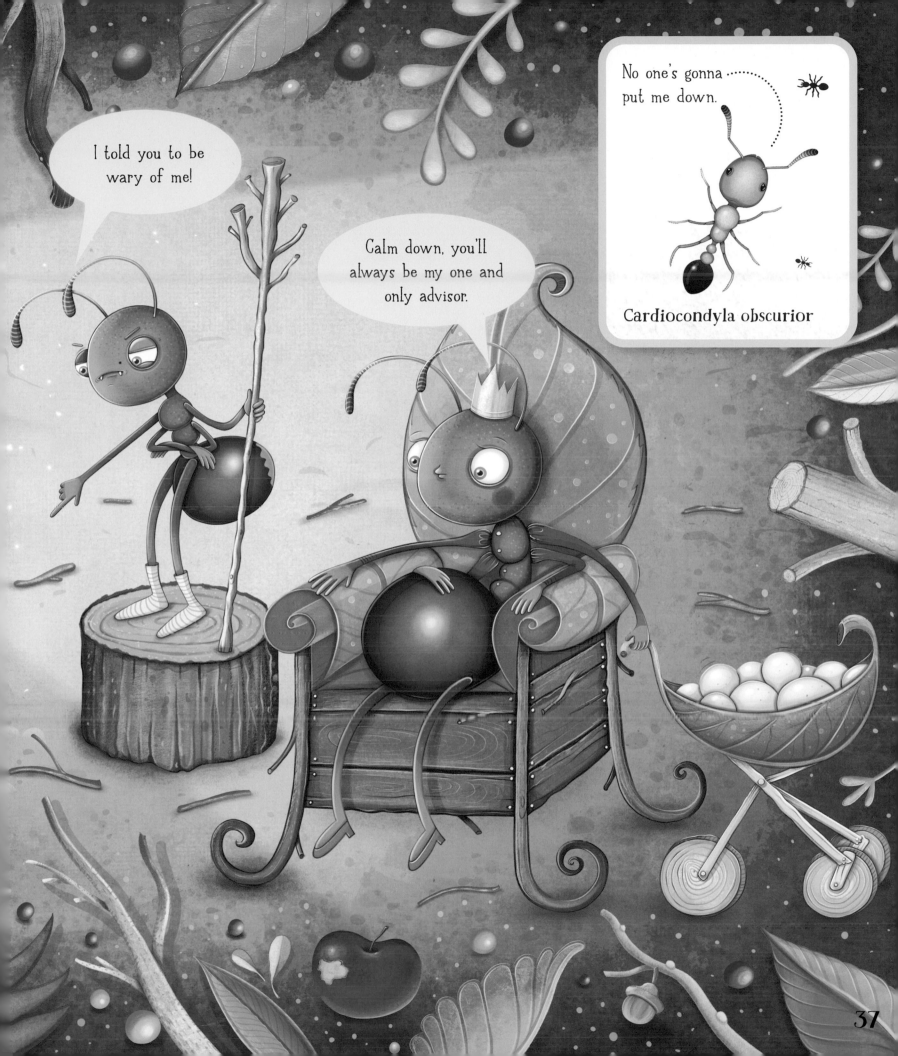

Big heads marching to a big battle

Numerous arrays of sinister African ants are marching through the land, destroying everything they come across. The front line is full of offending workers, and the rear consists of ants tasked with protecting future queens. Anywhere these noticeably large-headed ants appear, other insects vanish. That's because the ants are eliminating them on purpose, getting rid of their competition. How crafty, starving enemies out by depriving them of food.

Peep, there's nothing to eat around here

Contact with these ants can be fatal even to the much larger and much stronger birds. Before the songsters realize it, there's nothing for them to eat. That's because the quick ants manage to consume any and all insects far and wide.

Peep, I'm hungry.

My head is shaped like a heart.

Pheidole megacephala

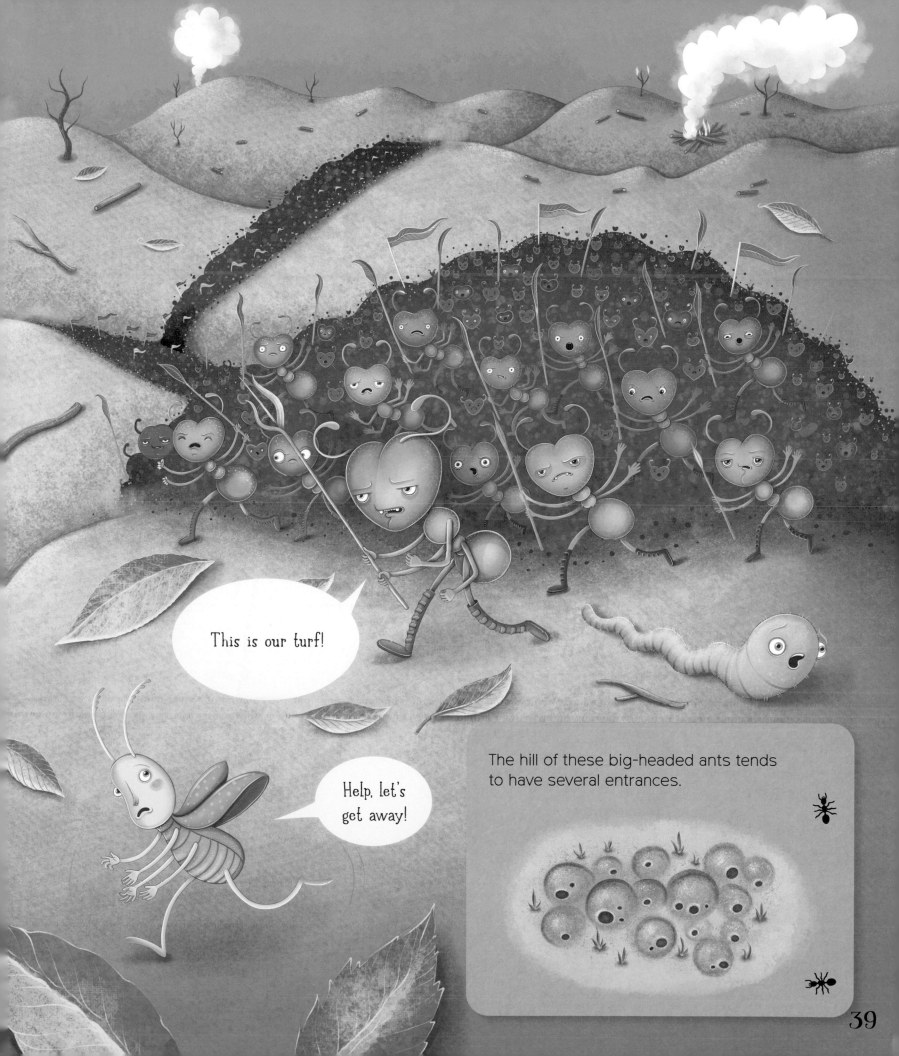

The hill of these big-headed ants tends to have several entrances.

39

First published as *World of Ants*
© Designed by B4U Publishing,
member of Albatros Media Group, 2023.
Author: Štěpánka Sekaninová
Illustrator: Zuzana Dreadka Krutá
www.albatrosmedia.eu

First Sky Pony Press edition, 2024

Sky Pony Press books may be purchased in bulk at special discounts for sales promotion, corporate gifts, fund-raising, or educational purposes. Special editions can also be created to specifications. For details, contact the Special Sales Department, Sky Pony Press, 307 West 36th Street, 11th Floor, New York, NY 10018 or info@skyhorsepublishing.com.

Sky Pony® is a registered trademark of Skyhorse Publishing, Inc.®, a Delaware corporation.

Visit our website at www.skyponypress.com.

10 9 8 7 6 5 4 3 2 1

Manufactured in China, January 2024
This product conforms to CPSIA 2008

Library of Congress Cataloging-in-Publication Data is available on file.

Cover design by Kai Texel
Cover illustrations by Zuzana Dreadka Krutá
US Edition edited by Nicole Frail

Print ISBN: 978-1-5107-7907-5
Ebook ISBN: 978-1-5107-7908-2